P9-CEL-536

SNOW LEOPARD

Written by
Jill Bailey

Illustrated by
Peter Bull Art Studio

GALLERY BOOKS
An Imprint of W. H. Smith Publishers Inc.
112 Madison Avenue
New York City 10016

This series is concerned with the world's endangered animals, the reasons why their numbers are diminishing, and the efforts being made to save them from extinction. The author has described these events through the eyes of fictional characters. Although the situations described are based on fact, the people and the events described are fictitious.

A Templar Book

First trade edition published in the USA in 1991 by GALLERY BOOKS, an imprint of W.H. Smith Publishers Inc., 112 Madison Avenue, New York, New York 10016.

First trade edition published in Canada in 1991 by W.H. Smith Ltd, 113 Merton Street, Toronto, Canada M45 1A8.

Gallery Books are available for bulk purchase for sales promotions and premium use. For details write or telephone the Manager of Special Sales, W.H. Smith Publishers, Inc., 112 Madison Avenue, New York, New York 10016. (212) 532-6600

Copyright © 1991 by The Templar Company plc

All rights reserved. No part of this publication may be reproduced, stored in a retrieval system, or transmitted in any form or by any means, electronic, mechanical, photocopying, recording or otherwise, without the prior permission of the publishers and copyright holder.

Devised and produced by The Templar Company plc, Pippbrook Mill, London Road, Dorking, Surrey RH4 1JE, Great Britain.

Color separations by Positive Colour Ltd, Maldon, Essex, Great Britain. Printed and bound by L.E.G.O., Vicenza, Italy

ISBN 0-8317-7831-8

CONTENTS

TRACKING THE SNOW LEOPARD

There was a commotion on the trail outside. **Karma** left his warm fire and went to investigate the noise. Several villagers were carrying the remains of a dead yak. They were singing because there was going to be a feast that night.

For the villagers of Namdo, high in the Himalayas of west Nepal, meat is a treat they can rarely afford, especially at the end of winter. The yaks are kept mainly for their milk, which is made into butter and cheese.

The dead yak must have met with an accident – there was no special reason for killing one. Thondup, the owner of the dead yak, was certainly not celebrating.

"What happened?" asked Karma.

"Snow leopard," snapped Thondup.

Karma recognized the yak by its crumpled horn. It was Thondup's oldest animal and had been ailing all winter. That was probably why the snow leopard, less than half the yak's size, had been able to kill it. Tiny puncture marks on the yak's neck revealed the leopard's swift killing method – a suffocating bite to the throat.

A figure pushed through the group towards Karma. It was his old friend, Lopsang.

"The leopard is hunting lower down the mountain than usual," Lopsang remarked. "With so much snow this winter, the high pastures are still covered. This could be a chance to make some money."

Left: snow leopards live in remote places high in the mountains of Central Asia. In winter, deep snow on the upper slopes forces them to hunt farther down the mountain.

Above: as villages expand and domestic animals are grazed on higher and higher slopes, the villagers come into contact with snow leopards more often.

Karma frowned. Lopsang was a skilled poacher and leopard skins could still bring a high price in the market at Jumla.

"It's illegal to kill snow leopards," said Karma. "You won't make much money if they catch you and make you pay a fine. You could even go to jail."

"Go to jail for killing a wild animal," scoffed Lopsang. "People of Namdo have been protecting

Local hunters are paid only about $30 for a snow leopard skin, yet this is almost a year's cash income to some of them. The temptation to hunt is very strong.

their yaks and goats against leopards for hundreds of years."

"It's only killed one old yak," said Karma. "The wolves take more animals, and you know that snow leopards never attack people."

Lopsang kicked a stone defiantly.

"What do those officials in Katmandu, with their electric lights and their running water, know about living in a place like this? Why in this village, only Sonam has a cassette, and there are only three radios in the whole village."

Lopsang was envious of Sonam's cassette player, and wanted desperately to earn enough money to buy one.

"It's all right for you," Lopsang complained. "You're going to earn good money working for Mr Cameron. What else can I do? Tomorrow I'm going after that leopard. Are you coming with me?"

Karma hesitated.

"I don't think so," he said at last.

"You have to," said Lopsang sharply. "If you don't come, how do I know you won't tell Mr Cameron? Then he'll tell the police? If you come with me, you won't be able to tell anyone."

"Okay," Karma sighed. He was unwilling to lose his old friend.

Domestic yaks graze the mountain grasslands. Snow leopards will not usually attack them so long as there are plenty of natural prey animals around.

9

Above: porters crossing a river by means of a log bridge. Karma often worked as a porter for tourists or researchers.

Right: Karma and Lopsang set off in search of the snow leopard. Karma was secretly hoping that they wouldn't find it.

10

Unlike most of the villagers, Karma often worked as a porter for tourist parties many miles from Namdo. Eager to learn, he had soon picked up enough English to be in demand. The previous year, he had met the big Scotsman, Cameron Douglas (Lopsang's "Missa Cameron"), who had come to study the blue sheep and the snow leopards of the Kandu valley, about a day's walk from Namdo. Cameron's companion, Rick Smith, had had to return to England unexpectedly, and Cameron had asked Karma to help him instead.

If Cameron found out that Karma was helping a poacher, he would lose his new job. Perhaps they would not find the snow leopard, or perhaps he could prevent Lopsang from killing it. Karma slept very badly that night.

Early the next morning, before the frost had left the rooftops, Karma and Lopsang set out into the mountains. The bushes were sprouting fresh green leaves and the peach trees were covered in soft pink blossoms. In the distance lay the snow-capped peaks of the high Himalayas. Karma and Lopsang headed for the place where the yak had been killed. Suddenly, Lopsang stopped and pointed.

"Tracks," he said. The prints of a leopard lay in the soft mud, where it had been disturbed by the villagers the day before. There were two sizes of prints; the larger were made by the big front paws. Karma and Lopsang followed the tracks higher and higher towards the towering cliffs above the Suli river.

Suddenly the tracks became confused. There were other tracks mixed up with them, the cloven hoof-prints of bharal, or blue sheep.

"The leopard must have disturbed the sheep as it fled from the villagers," remarked Lopsang. "Let's split up and see if we can pick up its tracks again." He began to search farther up the slope. Karma headed toward the nearby cliffs, knowing that this was the sort of place where the leopard might lie up during the day. Soon he found some tracks, but these were not the tracks of an adult snow leopard, they were too small. Cubs! They were probably about nine months old. That would be why the snow leopard had attacked the yak. Two romping cubs would soon scatter a herd of bharal, but the yaks were

Below: yaks carrying researchers' equipment into a study area. They are crossing a pass in West Nepal. The peaks of the Himalayas can be seen in the distance.

Right: the rugged nature of this mountain country has helped to save the snow leopard. The steep slopes are not suitable for growing crops or building homes.

less easily upset. Karma was very uneasy. He did not want the cubs to lose their mother.

Meanwhile, Lopsang had found the mother's tracks leading into the cliffs. He called to Karma to follow. The tracks led along a narrow ledge. Almost 3 hundred feet below them flowed the Suli river, roaring and foaming over treacherous boulders.

"This is getting too dangerous," warned Karma as small stones, loosened by the melting snow, bounced over their heads.

"We can't be far from the leopard's den," said Lopsang.

As he spoke, a large rock gave way under his foot and he began to slide. His other foot also slid off the ledge and he vanished from sight, screaming as he fell.

The stones stopped raining down, and Karma could once again hear the river roaring below him.

"Karma, I'm all right," shouted Lopsang. "Can you pull me up?"

Karma tiptoed to the edge of the ledge and saw Lopsang hanging on to a stunted juniper tree that was growing out of the rocks. He lay on the ground and stretched out his hand towards his friend.

"Don't look down, Lopsang," he ordered. "Take my hand and I'll pull you up. That tree won't hold you for much longer."

A few minutes later, Lopsang was stretched out on the grass beside Karma. His leg and hands were bleeding badly.

"I'm going home," he said.

"I'll stay here a bit longer," said Karma. "I'll catch up with you later."

As Lopsang disappeared down

Left: snow leopard country is rugged and dangerous. Even experienced hunters meet with accidents. Had he been alone, Lopsang might well have died. This is the reason why researchers and tourists rarely travel alone.

Right: snow leopards are very well camouflaged. Their soft, gray coats blend in with the rocks. The markings on their coats help to conceal the outlines of their bodies.

the mountainside, Karma gazed up the slope to where he had found the cubs' tracks. Then he got the feeling he was being watched. There, in the shadow of a rock, lay a misty grey animal, perfectly still, watching him with ice-blue eyes. It was the snow leopard. Karma marvelled at how well it blended into the landscape. Its fur was so soft that it seemed to melt into the mountainside.

There was a slight movement behind the leopard, and the small rounded ears of a cub came into view. It leapt over its mother and started down the hill toward Karma. In a flash the snow leopard sprang to its feet, and mother and cub vanished into the cliffs.

That night Karma lay awake, thinking about the snow leopard. Suddenly, the cries of a distressed goat pierced the night air. Karma leapt to his feet and rushed to the barn that formed part of the ground floor of his father's house. As he ran down the steps, a shadowy shape darted across the trail and vanished into the night. It was the snow leopard.

Other villagers were arriving, armed with sharpened bamboo spears and guns. They began to run after the snow leopard. Regardless of the law, it was customary to hunt down and kill a leopard that attacked animals in the village.

"No!" shouted Karma. "That was only a dog. The leopard went that

There are more people living in the mountains than ever before, and they graze their animals in snow leopard country. More and more snow leopards are being shot for attacking livestock.

way," and he pointed in the opposite direction.

To his relief, the crowd followed his pointing finger. The goat was bleeding but not seriously hurt, thanks to Karma's quick arrival on the scene. The leopard's claws had slashed its rump, but the wounds were not deep. The leopard had got in through the small shaft left for ventilation.

"I told father that hole was too big," muttered Karma. The next day he would fix bars across the hole. Karma felt almost sorry for the snow leopard. After all its efforts to kill the yak yesterday, the villagers had carried off its supper and the cubs were still hungry. He hoped that the snow would soon clear up, so that the leopard could reach its summer hunting grounds in the high alpine pastures.

Inside a village house. Mountain people live simply. These villages have no electricity and no running water.

LEOPARD COUNTRY

Cameron Douglas awoke to the welcoming smell of coffee brewing on the camp fire. His new assistant, Karma, certainly knew how to make himself useful. The camp was at the mouth of a cave high above the Kandu river, with a superb view of the valley and the hills opposite. In the distance the mist was starting to rise from the snow-capped mountain peaks.

Cameron reached for the radio antenna. Yesterday they had trapped a male snow leopard and fitted a radio collar around his neck.

Cameron wanted to see if the animal, whom he had named Zig, was still in the area. He pointed the antenna at the opposite cliff. There was no sound. He traced the track up the valley and suddenly he got a signal. "Beep! … Beep! … Beep!" It was a slow signal; the leopard was resting. This was not surprising. Snow leopards are usually most active around dawn and in the evening, and it was already 9 a.m. Cameron and Karma had slept late.

Cameron was trying to record the movements of the snow leopards of the Kandu valley.

Above: a researchers' camp high up in the mountains. From here they can track the leopards' movements.

Left: radio signals are easily blocked by quite small boulders. When trying to pick up signals, it is best to find a place high on the side of a cliff with good views all around.

He wanted to find out how far they traveled in a year. Then he would be able to work out how big a nature reserve would need to be to protect a reasonably large number of snow leopards. By trapping snow leopards and fitting them with collars that transmitted radio signals, he could follow their wanderings.

So far, Cameron had fitted collars to three snow leopards in the Kandu valley – two males and a female. The other male, Irbis, had wandered high up the valley out of the range of the radio receiver. Sabu, the female, had been quiet for several days now. Five days earlier, Cameron had picked up her signals near Eddu camp, on the opposite side of the valley. He decided to go there to see if she was still around.

Cameron and Karma set off down the valley. The Kandu river was rising rapidly as the snow melted, and the log bridge they

Snow leopards often use tracks made by blue sheep, or bharal. The leopards move quietly and stealthily to avoid being noticed.

had made would soon be washed away. There were snow leopard tracks in the soft mud of the river bank. The two men followed the tracks up the rocky hillside.

"The cat is using a bharal track," commented Karma.

"Yes," said Cameron, "but it will soon head for that high ridge. Snow leopards like to walk where they have a good view of their surroundings."

Sure enough, the tracks soon veered off into a jumble of rocks and stunted juniper trees. Cameron stopped by a large boulder, then bent down and sniffed the rock. Karma roared with laughter.

"The villagers warned me that you smelled rocks," he said.

"Come and see for yourself," said Cameron. "It smells of snow leopard. The leopard has sprayed the rock to mark it."

"Even the village dogs squirt their urine on rocks," said Karma. "How do you know it's a snow leopard?"

Snow leopards scrape and spray scent at regular places along their trails. The scent tells other snow leopards that this patch of mountain is occupied.

21

"The leopard's scent spray comes from a gland. It isn't urine." said Cameron. "The scent tells other leopards who has passed this way."

"Why would they want to know that?" asked Karma.

"Food for snow leopards is very scarce here," replied Cameron. "There are barely enough bharal and other animals to support all the snow leopards in this area. If they hunt too close together, they will soon run out of food, so they like to keep their distance. Of course, in the mating season, in late winter, the male and female snow leopards *want* to find each other. The scent marks can help them then, too."

Karma studied the rock with renewed interest. Pointing to some scrape marks on the ground, he asked, "Are these made by the leopard, too?"

"Yes," replied Cameron. "They also leave scratch marks on trees. They like to mark trees as well as rocks, and they often scrape near overhanging cliffs."

Karma began to hunt for more scrapes. Soon he found them, beside a boulder.

"It looks as if there are several scrapes here," he said.

"The leopards have favorite places for scent-marking and scraping," explained Cameron. "I've watched Irbis walking along

this trail. He stops at the same places each time. First he sniffs them, I suppose to see who else has passed this way. Then he adds another scrape or spray to them. Some scrape sites may have been used for many generations."

"So that's why you go around smelling stones," laughed Karma.

Left: Cameron and Karma found scrape marks in the soil beside a boulder. Snow leopards also rake their claws down tree trunks. The marks show where they have been.

Below: while traveling, snow leopards pause at large boulders and trees and at the foot of cliffs to see if any other snow leopards have left a scent mark.

About half a mile farther on, the trail led up some steep cliffs and Karma and Cameron lost it. Eventually they arrived at Eddu camp, which was really just a rough shelter behind a large boulder surrounded by thorn bushes. Cameron chose a high place to stand and got out the radio antenna. At first there was nothing then he picked up a signal from Sabu, the female leopard. It was a slow resting signal.

"Either the collar has fallen off and is just lying on the ground, or the leopard is resting up somewhere," he said. "I wonder … it's the right time of year … perhaps she has just given birth to cubs. She will not venture far, as she will need to suckle the cubs. They need a lot of milk when they are so young."

"The snow leopard that raided our goat pen had two cubs," said Karma. "Is that the usual number?"

"In the wild they usually have only two or three cubs," said Cameron, "but in captivity, when they are well fed, they may produce as many as five at a time."

Above: a researcher studies a bharal killed by a snow leopard. The information helps him to find out how leopards live.

Left: snow leopards breed quite slowly. They are not mature until they are three or four years old. In captivity a female will stop breeding before she is 15, but they live for only ten years in the wild.

The sun was warm, and they decided to walk on to the point where the Kandu joined the Suli river. The meeting points of valleys are some of the snow leopards' favorite scent-marking places, and Cameron wanted to set some new traps there. They set several traps, simple nooses that would trap just one paw without damaging it. Then they covered the traps with earth.

The sun was already setting when Cameron and Karma set out for home. They had only gone a few yards when Karma suddenly leapt in the air, clutching his foot and yelling in pain. He had stepped on a sharpened bamboo spear set in the ground where the trail narrowed.

"Poachers!" said Cameron.

The local poachers use such spears, tipped with poison, to trap bharal, and sometimes snow leopards. On these cliffs the trap must have been intended for the snow leopards.

"Could it be the work of your friend Lopsang?" asked Cameron.

Karma looked startled.

"I didn't know you knew about him," he said.

"You'd better get down to the river and clean that wound," said Cameron. "That must have been an old spear, or you would be dead by now."

The following day, the weather looked threatening. Clouds hung low over the mountains.

Bamboo spears tipped with poison. These spears are used by hunters to catch bharal. Poachers use them to catch snow leopards.

"We must go and check the traps we set earlier," said Cameron, looking anxiously at Karma's bandaged foot.

They made slow and painful progress to Eddu camp. Karma scanned the valley with Cameron's binoculars. Suddenly, he spotted a movement in the distance.

"Cameron," he shouted. "There's a leopard in that trap!"

When they reached the trap, the snow leopard was crouched low in the grass, snarling and spitting at them. The two men approached slowly but kept their distance.

"This is going to be difficult," said Cameron. "The snare has caught its hind foot, so it can still lash out with its front feet. You'd better go around the other side and distract it while I inject it with a tranquilizer."

Cameron cleaned the wound in Karma's foot. Both men knew that the poisoned spear had been set by Lopsang.

Cameron brought out a long pole with a syringe on the end. Karma crept around the far side of the leopard, then suddenly stood up and waved his arms. The snow leopard swung around toward him, and Cameron darted forward, jabbing at its flank with the needle. Suddenly, Karma staggered backward, clutching his arm. The snow leopard had slashed his arm with its claws.

By the time Cameron had put a crude bandage on Karma's wound the leopard was immobilized. Carefully they measured it from head to tail. It was a mature female. Karma marvelled at her long thick tail and amazingly soft warm fur.

"You can tell individual snow leopards by the markings on their

28

heads," said Cameron, as he extracted a small tooth. "This tooth will tell us the age of the animal." He injected a small amount of antibiotic to make sure the cat's mouth did not become infected. "What shall we call her? How about Ounce – that's another name for the snow leopard?"

"Sounds fine," said Karma, still nursing his injured arm.

Cameron tattooed a small number onto the leopard's ear. This would enable them to recognize her later. As the leopard lay quietly, Cameron checked her temperature and breathing, and fastened the collar firmly around her neck. The radio transmitter was barely 3 inches long, but if it stayed in place it would give out a strong signal for at least two years.

The tranquilizer that Cameron injected into the leopard would immobilize it for a short time only. This would enable him to study the animal. The leopard is not harmed by the drug.

The leopard's muscles began to tense. She was waking up. Quickly Cameron took the camera out of his bag to photograph the leopard. From a safe distance they watched as the leopard staggered unsteadily to her feet, tottered a few paces to the shade of a tree, and lay down.

"Now let's get you to the herbal doctor in Namdo," said Cameron, inspecting Karma's bleeding arm. "He will be able to give you

something for the pain and stop you from getting a fever."

By the time they reached Namdo, Karma was in pain and feeling rather sorry for himself. The family gave them a warm welcome, and after several bowls of home-brewed beer, called *chang*, they were feeling better. While Karma visited the herbal doctor, Cameron went in search of Lopsang. He was surprised Lopsang had not been in the welcoming party.

Lopsang looked very uneasy. He stared at the floor and shifted from foot to foot.

"You know what I think about your poaching," said Cameron quietly, "especially when innocent people get hurt."

When he heard this, Lopsang looked even more unhappy.

"I've come to make you an offer," Cameron continued. "Tom and Babs Burton will soon be coming from England to film the snow leopards, and we shall need an extra helper to carry the cameras."

Lopsang couldn't believe his ears. He had been expecting to hear Cameron say that he was going to the police. Instead, he had offered him a job. It didn't make sense.

"There's one condition," said Cameron. "If I find you have been hunting the leopards, the deal's off. Understood?"

Lopsang looked up and smiled. "Understood," he said.

Left: a researcher fits a radio collar to a tranquilized snow leopard. The collar is not uncomfortable.

Below: while it sleeps, the snow leopard curls its long tail around itself to keep it warm.

FILMING THE SNOW LEOPARD

Tom and **Babs Burton** gazed gloomily at the snow drifting past the tent. They had been in the Kandu valley for three months now, and all they had managed to film was the trapping of one snow leopard. Ounce had managed to get caught again. They had come to make a film about the snow leopards, but all attempts to lure them within reach of the cameras using tethered goats as bait had failed.

"How many snow leopards do you think there are in the valley, Cameron?" asked Babs.

"I'm not sure," replied Cameron. "We have put collars on five. That may well be all of them. Even in this part of Nepal, where there is plenty of prey for them, each leopard needs about 15 square miles to live in. One adult will eat about 20 to 30 bharal a year."

"What else do they eat?" Babs asked.

"Various kinds of wild goats and sheep, hares, marmots, even pheasants and snowcocks. In some places the smaller animals make up half their diet."

"Are there any other places where they are found?" asked Babs. She was wondering if they might do better filming somewhere else.

"Oh yes," said Cameron. "They are found all across the Himalayas from Afghanistan to China, but in

---

Below: snow leopards lie down to eat. If disturbed during the day, they return to the carcass at night.

32

Above: snow leopards share their home with many other animals including the Langur, or black-faced monkey, shown here.

most places they are thought to be even more scarce than here. Perhaps you could try the Soviet Union. There are snow leopards there, but they are secretive animals and not easy to film anywhere."

The goat grunted restlessly outside. It had stopped snowing.

They decided to try to get some still photographs of the snow leopard. Cameron had had some good results by setting up a camera near one of the leopards' favorite trails and laying a touch-sensitive pad on the ground, connected to the camera. When the leopard stepped on the trigger, the camera fired.

Tom, Babs, Cameron, and Karma set off up the valley. Lopsang had been sent to Namdo to get some rope Cameron needed to repair

Snow leopards are very difficult animals to study. By examining scrape-marks, droppings, and reports of sightings, scientists have figured that there may be 5,000 snow leopards living in the world.

the log bridge. Near Eddu camp Cameron spotted some vultures circling in the sky overhead.

"That could mean there is a leopard kill over there," he said.

Sure enough, they found a half-eaten bharal below some cliffs.

"The leopard will return to feed later," said Cameron. "This looks like a good place to get some photographs."

They set up the camera, then hurried back to camp. To their surprise, there was no sign of Lopsang. Karma was uneasy. Was Lopsang up to his old tricks?

"Why did you hire him?" he asked Cameron.

"It was a bit of a risk," admitted Cameron. "Your friend is the main threat to the snow leopards around here. I hope if he can find well-paid work that depends on not killing them, we might reform him. I have promised to see that he is taken on as a guide when the national park opens – he's a good tracker."

"But I thought Lopsang was against the park," said Karma.

A touch-sensitive pad is hidden under leaves and soil on one of the snow leopard's favorite trails. The pad is connected to the trigger of the hidden camera. In this way, the leopard takes its own picture.

Namdo and the Kandu valley were to become part of a new national park being set up by the Nepal government.

The villagers were afraid the park authorities would stop them from grazing their animals on the high pastures, hunting the occasional bharal, and collecting firewood.

"There are a lot of rumors going around," said Cameron, "but the park will be good for Namdo. The villagers will probably be allowed to hunt a certain number of bharal, and there will be new trees for firewood. The larger number of tourists will need porters and cooks,

and they will buy handicrafts from the villages."

"Why should more tourists come here?" asked Karma.

"Foreigners expect national parks to have beautiful scenery and lots of wildlife," said Cameron. "For Americans and Europeans, the bharal are fascinating animals, and so are the bearded vultures that

---

Tourists are attracted to the dramatic scenery and exotic wildlife of mountain nature reserves. Tourism brings money to mountain villages, reducing the need to hunt snow leopards.

feed on their carcasses. There is even a tiny chance that they will see a snow leopard."

"A very small chance," said Tom, ruefully.

Lopsang appeared out of the shadows, looking rather shaken.

"What's happened to you?" asked Babs.

Lopsang looked uncomfortable.

"You've been after the snow leopards, haven't you?" said Karma, accusingly.

"Yes," replied Lopsang, "but it's not what you think. I saw the vultures this morning, and I thought if I could find the kill, Mr Cameron would be pleased with me. So I went to look. I found a carcass below the cliffs, but as I got closer something odd happened."

Tom burst out laughing.

"I know what happened," he said. "You got your picture taken!"

They all began to laugh. Lopsang looked embarrassed as he remembered how he had jumped when the flash had gone off.

A snow leopard has taken its own picture as it moves stealthily through the dark. This leopard may well be returning to a kill it made earlier in the day.

There was an eerie cry outside. Cameron looked out into the night. As he did so another yowl echoed across the valley.

"There's a snow leopard out there calling for a mate," he said.

"In winter?" asked Babs.

"Yes," said Cameron. "The young won't be born for at least three months. Then they will be able to make the most of the summer."

Three months later, when the peach trees were bursting into blossom, Ounce's signals suddenly went quiet, just as Sabu's had done the year before. Cameron guessed it had been Ounce calling that

Snow leopards have large paws. This helps them as they travel over the ragged rocks and cliffs of their natural habitat.

winter's night. Tom and Babs were depressed. They had still not managed to film the snow leopards, so they had decided to take some shots of the bharal and the pika. They had gone to the high pastures, now free of snow, to film the bharal and their young. Hidden by a large boulder, the camera was whirring happily when suddenly a group of bharal came rushing over the hill in a state of blind panic. Behind them bounded a snow leopard. The bharal leapt toward the cliffs. The snow leopard followed. Then it saw the camera, and the people. It stopped dead in its tracks, its glassy blue eyes staring in amazement. It crouched low, ears flattened against its head, and seemed almost to fade into the mountainside. The camera continued to run. The leopard hissed in annoyance, then, at last it turned and fled.

It was a very happy pair of filmmakers that later returned to camp for a new roll of film.

In this part of the Himalayas, the wild blue sheep, or bharal, is the snow leopards' main prey. When the leopard attacks, the bharal head for the safety of the cliffs.

A year later, Tom and Babs were in Katmandu on their way home. They still had very little film of the elusive snow leopards. On their last day in Nepal, they filmed the markets where snow leopard skins were still sold.

Visiting one shop, they had discovered snow leopard skins

Above: although most countries in the world ban the import and export of snow leopard skins, they are still sold in back street markets.

Right: in captivity, snow leopards live happily in pairs, but in the wild they seldom meet, except for a brief period during the mating season.

selling for over $900, and finished coats for $48,000.

"That's a lot of money for a dead snow leopard," commented Tom. "Lopsang was getting only $30 for his efforts."

Most countries in the world forbid the import of snow leopard products. With that, and the public outcry against killing endangered animals, the trade is declining.

Tom and Babs were going home to Britain to film the snow leopards at Bradwell Zoo. The zoo had two pairs of leopards. One of the females was about to give birth, something they had been unable to film in the wild.

Later that week, they met the keeper at Bradwell Zoo.

"Zoos with snow leopards keep strict records of the young they produce," he told them. "We know the history of just about every captive snow leopard in the world."

"Will you be able to return them to the wild?" asked Babs.

"We would like to," said the keeper, "but there are many problems to overcome. Even if we just move them from one pen to another they take months to settle down. There is also the problem of teaching them how to catch their own prey. In England we are not allowed to feed them live animals."

One of the zoo's females had just given birth. Tom and Babs had set up a hidden camera in her den. The cubs were tiny, and still blind.

"They will open their eyes in about two weeks," said the keeper.

A month later the cubs were a delight to film, rolling and tumbling around, growling and hissing at each other. They were just growing their first teeth.

"When will they start to eat meat?" asked Babs.

"At about eight weeks old," replied the keeper. "They will still need their mother's milk until they are five months old. In the wild they would stay with her, while she teaches them to hunt, until they are about two years old."

The other pair of leopards at the zoo had no cubs, but they were always together, rubbing cheeks, grooming each other, and uttering strange plaintive cries, half miaow, half yowl.

"It's amazing how affectionate they are," said Tom, "considering that in the wild they live alone."

"They are very faithful mates," said the keeper. "The male won't look at another female, even if she wants to mate."

As they left the zoo for the last time, Tom and Babs looked back at the snow leopard pen. The two leopards were lying close together on the rocks high up at the back of the pen. Their incredible pale blue eyes gazed out across the zoo as if looking for the distant mountains of their natural home.

Left: snow leopards breed well in captivity, but they do not like being moved to new homes. This makes it difficult to move captive animals back to the wild.

Above: by setting up reserves to protect the snow leopard, some of the world's most beautiful mountain areas are also saved for future generations to study and enjoy.

SNOW LEOPARD
UPDATE

USSR

MONGOLIA

IRAN

CHINA

AFGHANISTAN

PAKISTAN

HIMALAYAN
MOUNTAINS   BHUTAN

NEPAL

Katmandu

INDIA

VIETNAM

BURMA

LAOS

BANGLADESH

THAILAND

Snow leopard
range

SRI LANKA

INDIAN OCEAN

KAMPUCHEA

44

Snow leopards live in harsh, mountain areas. In these places there are not enough prey animals to support large numbers of snow leopards. Until recently their mountain strongholds were protected because they were remote. Today, there are more people living in the mountains than ever before. They are cultivating the land higher and higher up the mountains, and so destroying the snow leopards' habitat. Their livestock are grazing closer to the snow leopards' haunts. They graze in places where the leopards' natural prey once grazed. The leopards are then forced to prey more and more on domestic animals and often have to be killed.

There are probably about 5,000 snow leopards living in the wild, and about 370 in zoos around the world. Most of the countries in which they live give them legal protection. If they are to survive, however, there is an urgent need to set up more nature reserves and national parks where their habitat can be preserved. By encouraging limited tourism, it is possible to bring income to these mountain villages. This will reduce the need for larger farms and further hunting.

LEOPARDS AT RISK

● The three species of leopards are all suffering from the loss of the wild places in which they live. It is the snow leopard that is in the greatest danger of becoming extinct.

● The clouded leopard lives in the dense mountain forests of Asia and Indochina. It is the smallest of the leopards, only 2 to 3 feet long, with a darker, browner coat than the snow leopard.

● The common leopard is the largest species, and the least endangered. It is $3^1/2$ to $6^1/2$ feet long, with a golden-brown coat and dense pattern of dark spots. It lives in a wide range of habitats throughout Africa and Asia, from tropical rainforests to dry savannahs, cold mountains, and even city suburbs.

INDEX